Alexander

by Iain Gray

WRITING to REMEMBER

79 Main Street, Newtongrange,
Midlothian EH22 4NA
Tel: 0131 344 0414
E-mail: info@lang-syne.co.uk
www.langsyneshop.co.uk

Design by Dorothy Meikle
Printed by Printwell Ltd
© Lang Syne Publishers Ltd 2024

All rights reserved. No part of this publication may be reproduced, stored or introduced into a retrieval system, or transmitted in any form or by any means (electronic, mechanical, photocopying, recording or otherwise) without the prior written permission of Lang Syne Publishers Ltd.

ISBN 978-1-85217-754-6

Alexander

MOTTO:
Fortiter (Boldly)
(MacAlister)

CREST:
An embowed and armoured arm,
the hand grasping a sword

TERRITORY:
Kintyre

Chapter one:

The origins of the clan system

by Rennie McOwan

The original Scottish clans of the Highlands and the great families of the Lowlands and Borders were gatherings of families, relatives, allies and neighbours for mutual protection against rivals or invaders.

Scotland experienced invasion from the Vikings, the Romans and English armies from the south. The Norman invasion of what is now England also had an influence on land-holding in Scotland. Some of these invaders stayed on and in time became 'Scottish'.

The word clan derives from the Gaelic language term 'clann', meaning children, and it was first used many centuries ago as communities were formed around tribal lands in glens and mountain fastnesses.

The format of clans changed over the centuries, but at its best the chief and his family held the land on behalf of all, like trustees, and the ordinary clansmen and women believed they had a blood relationship with the founder of their clan.

There were two way duties and obligations. An inadequate chief could be deposed and replaced by someone of greater ability.

Clan people had an immense pride in race. Their relationship with the chief was like adult children to a father and they had a real dignity.

The concept of clanship is very old and a more feudal notion of authority gradually crept in.

Pictland, for instance, was divided into seven principalities ruled by feudal leaders who were the strongest and most charismatic leaders of their particular groups.

By the sixth century the 'British' kingdoms of Strathclyde, Lothian and Celtic Dalriada (Argyll) had emerged and Scotland, as one nation, began to take shape in the time of King Kenneth MacAlpin.

Some chiefs claimed descent from ancient kings which may not have been accurate in every case.

By the twelfth and thirteenth centuries the clans and families were more strongly brought under the central control of Scottish monarchs.

Lands were awarded and administered more and more under royal favour, yet the power of the area clan chiefs was still very great.

The long wars to ensure Scotland's

independence against the expansionist ideas of English monarchs extended the influence of some clans and reduced the lands of others.

Those who supported Scotland's greatest king, Robert the Bruce, were awarded the territories of the families who had opposed his claim to the Scottish throne.

In the Scottish Borders country – the notorious Debatable Lands – the great families built up a ferocious reputation for providing warlike men accustomed to raiding into England and occasionally fighting one another.

Chiefs had the power to dispense justice and to confiscate lands and clan warfare produced a society where martial virtues – courage, hardiness, tenacity – were greatly admired.

Gradually the relationship between the clans and the Crown became strained as Scottish monarchs became more orientated to life in the Lowlands and, on occasion, towards England.

The Highland clans spoke a different language, Gaelic, whereas the language of Lowland Scotland and the court was Scots and in more modern times, English.

Highlanders dressed differently, had different

customs, and their wild mountain land sometimes seemed almost foreign to people living in the Lowlands.

It must be emphasised that Gaelic culture was very rich and story-telling, poetry, piping, the clarsach (harp) and other music all flourished and were greatly respected.

Highland culture was different from other parts of Scotland but it was not inferior or less sophisticated.

Central Government, whether in London or Edinburgh, sometimes saw the Gaelic clans as a challenge to their authority and some sent expeditions into the Highlands and west to crush the power of the Lords of the Isles.

Nevertheless, when the eighteenth century Jacobite Risings came along the cause of the Stuarts was mainly supported by Highland clans.

The word Jacobite comes from the Latin for James – Jacobus. The Jacobites wanted to restore the exiled Stuarts to the throne of Britain.

The monarchies of Scotland and England became one in 1603 when King James VI of Scotland (1st of England) gained the English throne after Queen Elizabeth died.

The origins of the clan system

The Union of Parliaments of Scotland and England, the Treaty of Union, took place in 1707.

Some Highland clans, of course, and Lowland families opposed the Jacobites and supported the incoming Hanoverians.

After the Jacobite cause finally went down at Culloden in 1746 a kind of ethnic cleansing took place. The power of the chiefs was curtailed. Tartan and the pipes were banned in law.

Many emigrated, some because they wanted to, some because they were evicted by force. In addition, many Highlanders left for the cities of the south to seek work.

Many of the clan lands became home to sheep and deer shooting estates.

But the warlike traditions of the clans and the great Lowland and Border families lived on, with their descendants fighting bravely for freedom in two world wars.

Remember the men from whence you came, says the Gaelic proverb, and to that could be added the role of many heroic women.

The spirit of the clan, of having roots, whether Highland or Lowland, means much to thousands of people.

Meanwhile, many families proudly boast the heraldic device known as a Coat of Arms, as featured on our front cover.

The central motif of the Coat of Arms would originally have been what was sometimes borne on the shield of a warrior to distinguish himself from others on the battlefield.

Not featured on the Coat of Arms, but highlighted on page three, is the family motto and related crest – with the latter frequently different from the central motif.

Clan warfare produced a society where courage and tenacity were greatly admired

Chapter two:

Feuds and vendettas

In its Anglicised form of the Gaelic 'MacAlisdair', the Alexander name features prominently in the high drama that is Scotland's historical record.

Originally derived from a Greek name meaning 'defender of men', it was popularised as a forename in Scotland in the eleventh century through the influence of Queen Margaret, consort of King Malcolm III.

Born in 1045 in the English territorial fiefdom of Wessex and canonised after her death in 1093 as Saint Margaret because of her many pious works, she had sought exile from her English homeland in Hungary for a time – and it was here that she first encountered the Alexander name.

Returned from exile, she married Malcolm III in 1070 and, enamoured with Alexander as a forename – later, in common with many other given names, to also become a surname – she gave her son, the future King Alexander I, the name.

Further ensuring its popularity, two other Scottish kings, Alexander II, who reigned from 1214 until 1249 and Alexander III, who reigned from 1249 until his death in 1286, also bore the name.

In its Gaelic form of 'MacAlisdair', denoting 'son of Alisdair' and also rendered in a rather bewildering number of spelling variations that include "MacAlester", the Alexanders step into the pages of history.

Recognised as a sept, or sub-branch, of Clan MacAlister, the Alexanders are entitled to share in the clan's honours that include the motto of 'Boldly' and crest of an embowed and armoured arm, the hand grasping a sword.

Also, as kinsfolk of the MacAlisters, the Alexanders shared in both their glorious fortunes and tragic misfortunes.

The main territory of the MacAlisters/Alexanders was the Kintyre peninsula, in Argyll, on the west coast and the 'Alasdair' from whom they take their name was the thirteenth century Alasdair Mòr, a great-grandson of one of the most colourful characters in the history of Scotland's western seaboard.

This was Somerled, and it is through their proud descent from him that a rich and heady brew of both Norse and Celtic blood courses through the veins of the MacAlisters/Alexanders of today.

By the mid-twelfth century, Somerled, or Somhairle, whose name means 'summer wanderer' or 'summer sailor', had carved out a vast west coast fiefdom that included the south isles from Bute to Ardnamurchan Point in addition to Kintyre, Argyll and Lorne.

Fiercely independent, he considered he owed allegiance to no-one, not least the king.

It was following the death of King David I in 1153 that the king's grandson, Malcolm, succeeded to the throne as Malcolm IV.

He inherited a troubled kingdom torn apart by not only internecine warfare on the mainland but the threat of invasion from the north by Vikings, who sacked Aberdeen in the same year that he succeeded to the throne, and invasion from the west in the form of Somerled.

A powerful group of ambitious magnates, mainly centred in the Moray area in the northeast of Scotland, resolved to depose Malcolm, replacing him with their own puppet king, and were joined in this bold venture by Somerled, who was always eager to exploit any opportunity for warfare and plunder.

In 1157, he seized control of the islands of Bute and Arran and Malcolm sought to resolve the problem by ordering him to surrender his domains into the hands of the Crown, thereafter holding them as a mere vassal.

Somerled's answer was predictable: he assembled a 15,000 strong force of kinsmen and, embarking in a fleet of 164 swift galleys, sailed up the Firth of Clyde and then up the River Clyde to sack the town of Glasgow in a blood-crazed orgy of arson, rape and plunder.

Malcolm's loyal magnate in the west, Walter Fitzalan, the High Steward, hastily assembled a rag-tag force of other magnates and their retainers and Somerled met the woefully inadequate royal army at Renfrew.

Accounts differ on what now actually transpired on that bitterly cold day of January 1, 1164, but one account is that a fierce battle ensued and, as Somerled's battle-hardened Islesmen rapidly gained the upper hand over the royal forces, the tide of battle turned when Somerled received a mortal thrust from a spear.

Dismayed at the loss of their leader, the Islesmen's discipline broke down, and hundreds were slaughtered as they fled back to their galleys.

Somerled's domains subsequently split up

among his sons, and through this he is recognised as the progenitor, or founder, of the mighty MacDonald Lords of the Isles.

His great-grandson, Alasdair Mòr, who gave his name to the MacAlisters, was the son of Donald of Islay, Lord of the Isles, and a grandson of Somerled, and it was through this that the MacAlisters became a cadet branch of the MacDonalds – more properly known as Clan Donald – although they soon became established as a clan in their own proud right.

In one of the many internecine clan feuds and vendettas, Alasdair Mòr, whose name first appears in the historical record in 1253, was killed in 1299 in battle against Alasdair McDougall, Lord of Lorne, and succeeded by Domhnall, one of his five sons.

The MacAlisters/Alexanders became firmly established on the Kintyre peninsula, with the main branches through time being the MacAlisters of Tarbert, who served until 1706 as constables of Tarbert Castle, on Loch Fyne, the MacAlisters of Loup, whose seat was on the south shore of West Loch Tarbert and the Alexanders of Menstrie, Clackmannanshire.

In 1481, Charles MacAlister received a

sizeable grant of lands after James III appointed him Steward of Kintyre.

Later, in his rather self-important manual on kingship known as *Basilicon Doron* (Royal Gift), written in about 1599, James VI (later James I of England), expressed in no uncertain terms his fear and loathing for his subjects on the far-flung Western Isles of Scotland.

About 100 years earlier, in 1493, the situation had already reached such a stage of anarchy, with royal authority being flouted at every turn, that James IV annexed the Lordship of the Isles to the Crown, with the monarch himself assuming the title of Lord of the Isles.

But, nearly 100 years later, this had done little to curb the feuding, and James VI thundered that the unruly Islesmen such as the MacAlisters/Alexanders, were no better than wolves and wild boars.

So cruel were they in exacting revenge, the monarch claimed, that "neither have they regard to person, age, time or cause". In all respects, James summed up in *Basilicon Doron*, the Islesmen were "the most barbarous people that had ever been seen since the beginning of the world".

While the king painted a grossly exaggerated portrait of his Western subjects, there was some basis of truth to some of his claims.

In 1572, the Clan Chief of the MacAlisters, John MacAlister, was ordered by an Act of Parliament to deliver hostages 'for the security of his peaceable behaviour'.

In 1598, Godfrey MacAlister of Loup, for reasons that remain unclear, arranged for the murder of his former guardian and tutor, while in 1603, Archibald MacAlister of Tarbert, along with Campbell of Auchinbreck, led a force of 1,200 men who invaded and ravaged the Isle of Bute.

When not engaged in fighting one another throughout their own domains, the Islesmen were only too eager to lend their fighting support to their Gaelic counterparts in Ireland, the MacDonnells, as they resisted the power of the English Crown.

One MacAlister, killed in battle in Ulster in 1571, was recorded by the victorious English as having been "Owen McOwen duffe McAlastrain, called the Lord of Loup."

Following what is known as the Glorious Revolution of 1688 that brought William of Orange and his wife Mary to the thrones of England and

Alexander

Scotland, John Graham of Claverhouse, Viscount Dundee, raised the Royal Standard in favour of the exiled Stuart monarch James VII and II.

Gathering a 2,500-strong force of clansmen that included a contingent of MacAlisters led by Alexander MacAlister of Loup, he engaged a 4000-strong government force under General Hugh Mackay of Scourie at the Pass of Killiecrankie on July 27, 1689.

Both sides suffered terribly in the battle and the outcome proved to be inconclusive.

Alexander MacAlister of Loup survived the carnage and, along with what was left of his kinsfolk, escaped to Ireland, where he sided with the Jacobites against the forces of William of Orange in what is known as *Cogadh an Dá Rí*, or The War of the Two Kings.

It ended when the Jacobite and Williamite forces finally clashed on the morning of July 12, 1690, in the battle of the Boyne; the Jacobites were routed but, again, Alexander MacAlister of Loup survived.

Another important branch is the MacAlisters of Glenbarr, but it is the MacAlisters of Loup who are today recognised as the principal line with, at the time of writing, William St John Somerville McAlester of Loup and Kennox recognised as Chief of the Name and Arms of MacAlister.

His Gaelic title is Mac Iain Dubh, while the clan's historic seat is now Kennox House, situated between Torranyard and Stewarton, in North Ayrshire.

This came about when Charles McAlester, the only son of the then Clan Chief, Angus MacAlester of Loup, succeeded to his father's title in 1797, five years after having married Janet Somerville, whose father, William Somerville, had succeeded to the Kennox estate in 1743.

Alexander

Chapter three:

High office and honours

One important cadet branch of Clan MacAlister is the Alexanders of Menstrie, whose seat was Menstrie Castle, Clackmannanshire.

Known as the House of Alexander, they rose to prominence through the courtier William Alexander, born in Menstrie in about 1567.

Having received the trusted post of Gentleman Usher to Prince Charles – son of James I of England and James VI of Scotland and the future King Charles I – Alexander became such a loyal favourite of James, also serving as his private secretary and as a member of the Scottish Privy Council, that in 1621 he was granted a special royal charter.

This gave him lordship on behalf of the Crown over what was then the colony of Nova Scotia (New Scotland), in present day New Brunswick, Canada and, in addition to this vast territory he was granted control over parts of what is now the northern United States.

Created Lord Alexander of Tullibody and

Viscount of Stirling in 1630, he was further ennobled three years later under King Charles I as 1st Earl of Stirling; also an accomplished poet and dramatist, he died in 1640.

A Scots-American major-general during the American Revolutionary War of 1775 to 1783, his namesake William Alexander laid claim to the title of Lord Stirling through his Scottish lineage.

It was as the senior male descendant of the paternal grandfather of the 1st Earl of Stirling that he staked his claim.

But, initially granted the title by a Scottish court in 1759, it was later overturned by the House of Lords – despite having been ruled valid under Scots law.

Having commanded the 1st Maryland Regiment at the battle of Long Island, also known as the battle of Brooklyn Heights, in 1776 and captured by the victorious British, he died in 1783.

Back on British shores and in the world of politics, Albert Alexander, 1st Earl of Alexander of Hillsborough, was the British Labour Co-operative politician who held a number of high government offices.

Born in 1885 in Weston-super-Mare,

Somerset, the son of a blacksmith and a corset-maker, the family moved to Bristol when he was an infant, following the death of his father.

Joining the Western Co-operative Society when he was aged 23 and, later, his local Trades and Labour Council, he was elected Member of Parliament (MP) for Sheffield in 1922.

Only two years later, under the first Labour government, Prime Minister Ramsay MacDonald appointed him Parliamentary Under-Secretary to the Board of Trade, while subsequent positions of high office included First Lord of the Admiralty, during the Second World War and, later, Minister of Defence.

Stepping down from politics in 1950, by which time he had been raised to the peerage as Viscount Alexander of Hillsborough, he was further honoured two years before his death in 1965 as Earl Alexander.

In contemporary British politics, Danny Alexander, now more formally known as Sir Daniel Alexander, is the British former Liberal Democrat politician born in Edinburgh in 1972.

Elected Liberal Democrat MP for the Scottish seat of Inverness, Nairn, Badenoch and Strathspey in 2005, posts he held include Liberal

Democrat Shadow Secretary for Works and Pensions and, between 2005 and 2010, during the coalition government of the Conservative Party and the Liberal Democrats, Chief Secretary to the Treasury.

Chief of staff to former Liberal Democrats' leader Nick Clegg, he stood down from politics in 2015 and, knighted in that year, later took on the post of vice president and corporate secretary of the Asian Infrastructure Bank.

Born in Glasgow in 1967, Douglas Alexander is the Labour Party politician who represented the Scottish constituency of Paisley South from 1997 to 2005 and Paisley and Renfrewshire South from 2005 to 2015.

Positions he held under former Labour Prime Ministers Tony Blair and Gordon Brown include Secretary of State for Scotland, Secretary of State for Transport, Minister of State for Europe and Secretary of State for International Development.

His older sister Wendy Alexander, born in 1963, is the former Labour Party politician who held the seat of Paisley North, and later Paisley and Renfrewshire South as a Member of the Scottish Parliament (MSP).

Having served in posts outwith government

that include Vice-Principal (International) of Dundee University, she was elected a Fellow of the Royal Society of Edinburgh in 2016 in recognition of her work for the university sector.

Returning to the battlefield, Field Marshall Hugh Alexander, 1st Earl Alexander of Tunis, was the highly decorated British Army officer of Ulster-Scots descent born in London in 1891 to a family with a long aristocratic pedigree.

The third son of James Alexander, 4th Earl of Caledon and the Countess of Caledon, a daughter of the 3rd Earl of Norbury, he was married to Lady Margaret Bingham, daughter of George Bingham, 5th Earl of Lucan.

Entering the Royal Military College, Sandhurst, when he was aged 20, he gained great distinction in both the First and Second World Wars.

Commissioned a second lieutenant in the Irish Guards on the outbreak of the first conflict in 1914 and serving on the Western Front, he rose rapidly through the ranks to lieutenant-general – having taken part in the retreat from Mons in 1914, the Battle of Loos a year later and the battle of the Somme in 1916.

A recipient of both the Military Cross (MC) for his bravery at Loos and the Distinguished Service

Order (DSO) for his operations during the Somme offensives, his actions during the Second World War were no less distinguished.

Commanding the 15th Army Group as it fought its way through German-occupied Italy – from the 'toe' of the country all the way north to Rome – in some of the most bloody and protracted engagements of the war, he had also commanded actions during the North Africa campaign.

By now with the rank of Field Marshall, he was elevated to the peerage in 1946 as Viscount Alexander of Tunis – in recognition of the battles for Tunis during the North Africa campaign.

Also appointed Knight Grand Cross of the Order of Saint Michael and Saint George, and serving for a time as Chief of the Imperial General Staff and also Governor General of Canada, he died in 1969.

Chapter four:

On the world stage

From the stage and music to art and the complex realm of code-breaking, bearers of the Alexander name have gained acclaim through a diverse range of endeavours and pursuits.

On the stage, Jay Scott Greenspan is the American actor, voice actor, comedian and singer better known as **Jason Alexander**.

Born in 1959 in Newark, New Jersey, his best known role is that of George Costanza in the television series *Seinfeld*, which has won him three Golden Globe Awards.

Big screen credits include the 1990 *Pretty Woman*, while on the Broadway stage he is the recipient of a Tony Award for Best Leading Actor in a Musical for his role in a 1989 production of *Jerome Robbin's Broadway*.

Not only an American actor, singer, dancer and set designer but also a noted photographer, Allen Smith, better known by his stage name **Cris Alexander** was born in 1920 in Tulsa, Oklahoma.

A star of Broadway, his credits include

membership of the original cast of Leonard Bernstein's 1944 musical *On the Town*, *Present Laughter* and *Wonderful Town*.

Having appeared in the original production of *Mame*, he reprised his role in its 1958 screen adaptation, *Auntie Mame*.

Having set up his own photographic studio in New York, he took portraits of a number of celebrities, worked as a photographer for pop artist Andy Warhol and as chief photographer for New York City Ballet.

He met his partner Shaun O'Brien, a dancer with the ballet company, in the late 1940s, and the couple married in 2011 when same-sex marriage became legal in New York State – only a year before Alexander died.

On British shores, **Jean Alexander** was the actress best known for her role from 1964 until 1987 of Hilda Ogden in the long-running television soap *Coronation Street* – and for which she won the 1985 Royal Television Society Award for Best Performance.

Born Jean Mavis Hodgkinson in Toxteth, Liverpool, in 1926, other television credits before her death in 2016 include *Last of the Summer Wine*.

From the stage to music, **Tom** and **Jack**

Alexander

Alexander were the popular Scottish folk music duo known as the **Alexander Brothers**.

Tom, born in 1934 in Cambusnethan, North Lanarkshire and his younger brother Jack, born a year later, began music lessons at an early age, with Tom showing aptitude for the accordion and his brother the piano.

Eventually abandoning their day jobs as painters and decorators as their popularity grew while playing a number of venues, they were offered a recording contract and their song *Nobody's Child*, released in 1964, even out-sold the Beatles in Scotland.

Touring the United States, Canada, Australia and New Zealand, further hit recordings followed including *Bonnie Wee Jeannie McColl*, *These Are My Mountains* and *The Northern Lights of Old Aberdeen*.

Awarded MBEs in 2005 for their contribution to music, Jack died in 2013 and Tom in 2020.

On a decidedly religious musical note, **Cecil Frances Alexander** was the Anglo-Irish hymn writer and poet whose legacy survives to this day through a number of instantly-recognisable hymns.

Born in Dublin in 1818 and already known as a hymn writer in her teenage years, later compositions include *There is a Green Hill Far Away*, the Christmas Carol *Once in Royal David's City* and *All Things Bright and Beautiful*.

Married to the Anglican Church clergyman William Alexander, Bishop of Derry and Archbishop of Armagh, she died in 1895.

Bearers of the Alexander name have also excelled in the creative world of art.

Born in Glasgow in 1896, **Ann Dunlop Alexander** was the Scottish artist who specialised in watercolours and oils, in addition to designing ceramics and illustrating books – with myths and legends two of her main inspirations.

Her work having been exhibited at the Royal Glasgow Institute of Fine Arts and the Royal Scottish Academy, she died in 1969.

In much earlier times, **John Alexander** was the Scottish painter, engraver and staunch Jacobite – those who sought the restoration to the throne of the Royal House of Stuart – in Aberdeen in 1686.

The son of a doctor, he travelled to Rome in 1711 to study under the renowned Italian artist Giuseppe Chiara and, while there, executed a number of commissions for the Stuart court in exile.

Taking part in the abortive 1745 Jacobite

Rising that ended in the carnage of the battle of Culloden, he fled into exile but returned later to resume his artistic career, while many of his famous portraits include John Graham, 1st Viscount Dundee.

He died in 1766, while his son **Cosmo Alexander** took up his mantle both as an artist and Jacobite.

Born in 1724, he took exile in Rome in 1747, and it was here that he executed his iconic portrait of Charles Edward Stuart – better known to posterity as Bonnie Prince Charlie; later returning from exile, he died in 1772.

In more contemporary times, **Lena M. Alexander**, later also known by her married name of Lena Duncan, was the Scottish artist noted for her portrait and flower paintings.

Born in Glasgow in 1899 and a graduate of Glasgow School of Art, she moved to Kirkcudbright, in the southwest of Scotland, and was a member of the Kirkcudbright School of Artists.

A regular exhibitor at the Royal Scottish Academy and with works that include *Still Life in the Twentieth Century*, she died in 1983.

In the world of science, **Claudia Alexander**, born in Vancouver in 1959 and who died in 2015, was the Canadian-born American geophysicist and planetary scientist who, as a member of NASA's Jet Propulsion Laboratory team, was a project manager for the agency's 1989 Galileo mission to Jupiter.

One particularly cerebral bearer of the Alexander name was Conel Hugh O'Donel Alexander, better known as **Hugh Alexander** and by his pen-name C.H. O'D. Alexander.

Born into an Anglo-Irish family in Cork in 1909 and a mathematician, he was one of the highly select team who worked as a cryptanalyst at Bletchley Park, Buckinghamshire, during the Second World War decoding the German Enigma machine used for military communications.

Later the head, for 25 years, of the cryptanalysis section at the Government Communications Headquarters (GCHQ), Cheltenham, he was also a British chess champion and winner of the International Master title in 1950.

He died in 1974 and was portrayed by the actor Matthew Goode in the 2014 film *The Imitation Game*, based on Bletchley Park.

His son **Sir Michael Alexander**, born in Hampshire in 1936, was the British diplomat who served as foreign policy secretary to former Prime

Minister Margaret Thatcher and UK Ambassador to NATO and to Austria.

He died in 2002, while his brother **Patrick Alexander**, born in 1940, was the poet who, after settling in Australia and with works that include his 1976 *Throwing Shadows*, was renowned as a performance poet; he died in 2005.

From science to sport, **John Alexander** is the Australian politician and former professional tennis player born in Sydney in 1951.

As a player, he was ranked 8th in the men's world singles rankings in 1975 and was also a member of the Australian team that won the Davis Cup in 1977; now focussing on politics, he is a member of the Australian Liberal Party.

One particularly enterprising bearer of the Alexander name was Bertha 'Beatrice' Alexander Behram, better known to generations of doll lovers as **Madame Alexander**, founder of the Alexander Doll Company.

Born in 1895 in New York City to Russian-Jewish immigrants and adopting her stepfather Maurice Alexander's name after her father died, she worked with her stepfather in a 'doll's hospital' he had set up, repairing porcelain dolls.

She had also, along with a sister, helped to craft dolls to be sold in the hospital, and she proved to be so creative and proficient that by 1923 she had established her own Alexander Doll Company – a business that expanded so rapidly it became one of the leading doll manufacturers in the USA.

Fashioning accurately detailed dolls by researching historical dress and clothing and dressing them in 'silks, satins and other fine fabrics', her dolls were unique – with many of her collections based on celebrities and characters from popular books and films.

Cannily obtaining trademarks to manufacture dolls of famous people such as Jacqueline Kennedy, she also produced a collection of 36 dolls, complete with authentic outfits, to replicate the royal family and guests at the coronation in 1953 of Queen Elizabeth II.

Staying on as a design consultant after selling her business in 1988, she died two years later and was posthumously inducted into the Toy Industry Hall of Fame, while in 2013 the Alexander Doll Company issued a special Madame Alexander doll in her likeness and dressed in the style of the 1920s.